WOMAN LASSOS UNIVERSE

Woman Lassos Universe

*Poetic Expressions of Female Spirituality,
Adversity, and Empowerment*

KIRI JOHNSON

RESOURCE *Publications* • Eugene, Oregon

WOMAN LASSOS UNIVERSE
Poetic Expressions of Female Spirituality, Adversity, and Empowerment

Resource Publications
An Imprint of Wipf and Stock Publishers
199 W. 8th Ave., Suite 3
Eugene, OR 97401

www.wipfandstock.com

PAPERBACK ISBN: 979-8-3852-5708-9
HARDCOVER ISBN: 979-8-3852-5709-6
EBOOK ISBN: 979-8-3852-5710-2

VERSION NUMBER 10/02/25

To my children; my purpose, my blessing, my honour.
Keep being the light.

To Wendy Joy, the songbird who weaved wildness into us all.

And to my pops, whose bravery and unwavering morality
inspires me every day. With extended gratitude for the
exceptionality of organ donors and the NHS for making
our revitalised shared time possible.

CONTENTS

BLACK AND WHITE

Perhaps amidst the poison mist
clouding it, there was a seedling
of truth to your words of blade -
honesty hissing through coiled tongues.

Perhaps your demonic desires
to destroy it allowed you to
truly know it, intrinsically.
The closest of enemies.

Perhaps you played heart roulette
enough times to perceive its
kaleidoscope of emotions.
Captivating, yet changeable.

Perhaps I love-fooled my own heart
by seeking to define it
and all along you were right -
love is not black and white.

BEFORE: A MESSAGE

There are impact moments in life
that, even as they are happening,
you know will forever change you.

Life will now be separated
by invisible thorned thread
into before and after.

Before the diagnosis and
after; before the phone call and
after; before them and after.

The wisdom of After reflects
on the innocence of Before
with a mixture of sadness and pride -

and a vision of sharing a quiet
moment in indistinct space and time
to comfort and prepare the bright,

unsuspecting soul for the
agony it's about to endure.
One day the cloud will lift and

peace will infiltrate cells where
armoured energy once pounded
the walls. An internal ceasefire.

Creating capacity for
contemplation of how you made it
through a war you swore would destroy you.

And you will begin to wonder
whether After's message for Before
was soul-imbedded all along.

Through expanded timelines and shifting
dimensions: the guiding light
was the strength of your future self.

TIMELESS LOVE

It has nothing to do with how long you are partnered,
how many years you've conquered
or how brimming the gathering of paper, diamond, gold
in your anniversary keepsake box.

Love cannot be quantified by time,
since time is a construct, and love knows no bounds.
To codify love is to catch fireflies in a fishing net -
their glow will infuse space long after the midnight hour.

Love cannot hear ticking, nor does it chase the clock.
If Cupid is shy of the mark in this life, he will sharpen his arrow
and hit the bullseye in the next, or the next.
There is no timepiece on Earth more precise than divine timing.

Be receptive of love at first sight and, 'I don't even know you'.
Trust energy recognition, since energy travels faster than all that is
quantifiable. Unconditional love transcends timelines;
speaking intuitively, not logically. Listen carefully.

SUNRISE

Raise your sparkling flutes to the sun -
it's supposed to be fun, this game.
Life is a manifestation

of abundant love, and love is
happy at its core. There is a
reason low residing people

are miserable. In simple terms,
happiness is a mindset, and
the fundamental principle

of the perspective of joyful
states is to surrender to love.
Leave this world smiling, remembered

for your magic, your alchemy
of grey into gold, and how you
danced across the sky like sunrise.

ANT COLONY

Close to the core there are colonies
of mating males who valiantly
ride then die.

In their wake, undeterred females. Queens
and workers, produce and nurture the
seed of life.

Suppose that one day the colony
wakes up and begins to question the
grand purpose.

Tired of void hedonism, male ants
yearn for life beyond systematic
procreation,

and a more heartfelt role in presence.
Valued for essence, as opposed to
provision:

true esteem over necessity,
soft memories over martyrdom.
Enmeshment

with species female - herself tired of
labouring for love. Mineral Huntress,
Godiva

of Darkness. Silenced below soil, where
few jobs are shared under the weight of
compliance.

Suppose this cardinal call from source
is Gaia placing a delicate
finger on

a festering nest. Matriarchs watch
and wait in patriarchal tunnels,
excited

to step into the light. While outside,
hunter gatherers - though some, 'not all' -
frantically

run in every direction. Fearing
change, soldered to comforting social
scaffolding,

struggling to accept the requisite -
despite dual deep-rooted entrapment -
for the shift.

When energies settle and the hand
lifts at divine - will past lessons be
wholly learned?

Past power relinquished? Past beliefs
updated? Will we finally be on
level soil?

THE WOMAN AT THE CROSS

It is a woman who pulls
the feet of Jesus downwards
as he is nailed to the cross
to bring an end to his pain.

The ultimate act of love.
Her misery as witness
marred across her tear-smeared face
as wails resound dusty dunes.

Grief overridden only
by her need to end his plight.
Fight mode activated, she
hangs her full weight from his legs,

pleading to heaven. Far from
half-hearted. Rapt - resolute -
she mind blocks from processing
the torture she's inflicting

on her beloved twin. This is
the only way for union
divine - flamed female saviour,
veiled healer Magdalena.

FEMININE RISING

If women were to direct as much energy
into loving themselves
as they do to emotionally scant men,
society would be brimming
with extraordinarily thriving females,

extending unwavering love freely
to every relationship they cultivate.
So balanced and boundless would this love be
that no perceivable distinction would exist
between male and female recipients.

So robust and moral that mirror males
would have no choice but to rise
to meet the conditions of her loving sphere -
triggering a necessary code of
introspection and healing,

instead of enabling toxic behaviour
rooted in unconscious fear and lack.
Women have long accepted the narrative
that they are dutybound to nurture men
to emotional prime. That male hostility

and avoidance are fixed obstacles
for *her* to absorb and overcome.
Be patient and forgiving with his primal
shortcomings: emotional maturity gap -
cut him some slack.

The first step in breaking
this karmic societal loop
is for women to empower
themselves as Goddesses
to the throne of consciousness.

Saving sacred space only
for masculine energies
that compliment her feminine.
Planting wildflower seed for flourishing
relationships of attuned polarities.

It is the female essence of Mother Nature
that is rising now; the awakened woman
must be the one to set the bar. Assured
in the knowledge that the moon doesn't demand
collaboration from the Sun. It just is. Balance.

NATURE'S SOPRANOS

Birds are supremely intuitive animals, funnelling one another's energy
as if sharing a universal vein. Never missing a beat, alive with vibrations
of the sky, synchronised with the secret of existence. Greeting each new
day with song - a melodic release of sacred morning energy.

Simply existing, impressing no one, for what is ego to a bird? Repelled
by the illusory pull of the physical plane, its instinct is to soar
upwards towards paradise. A peace reached by sweeping salvation
from dense superficiality. You've contemplated flight -

I know - I was born to birdsong. But humans will never
be as free as birds. It's not our destiny, since the sky is not our home.
Love keeps us rooted to the ground - the anchor of human existence,
fixing us to the Earth's core.

And with love comes responsibility. We are obligated to remain
and nourish our earthly connections, because our entanglements
with one another - beautiful, intrinsic, toxic - are essential
on our journey of enlightenment.

So we stay and watch birds fly, mesmerised by their liberation. Wondering
why we must suffer for the fruits of divinity, when it beads from seraph

feathers as air. Sometimes it would be easier to feel nothing, yet endurance is the price we pay for emotional fulfilment.

Soak in the ancient pearls of *Amor Fati* : love your fate. Delve deeper than acceptance and gratitude for lessons amassed - wholeheartedly adore every millstone weightily endured on your path to oneness. Drown in your miraculous metamorphosis.

The human experience is difficult by nature, because the rewards are so sublime. Birds cannot communicate love, but delight in signalling to its origins. So perhaps birds are messengers - healing energy angels - to guide our eyes to higher love.

Majestic reminders to look up for the answers, when bowing to the heaviness of this mortal experience seems inevitable. Graceful songbirds, nature's sopranos, thank you for the show.

PARAMOUNT LOVE

Your loving connections are paramount:
everything else must mould around them.
Unconditional love transcends galaxies,
time zones and existence. Therefore,
have no doubt that it will prevail across
separate homes and every other weekends.
These matrix paradigms that consume you
are your limitations. Superficial constructs:
mortgages, businesses, picture perfect lives -
so irrelevant that they are undetectable
to the awakened eye. When you break away
and lean into surrender of the divine plan,
you will be supported in discovering that
that the foundational elements required
to support your shift towards peace
will fall at your feet. You will magnetise
abundance. Such is the reward
for your enmeshment with the cosmos.
For relinquishing control. It was all
an illusion anyway. The proof?
Cast your mind back. You will realise
that every decision you have ever made
out of alignment with authentic love
has derailed or destroyed your happiness.
Love always wins.

WONDERLAND WHALE

All that vibrates with the energy
of the universe is true
reality: divine clarity.

Imagine if the atoms of
every material construct
were to dissolve to complete

transparency before your mind:
houses, roads, pavements, fences,
cars, telephone wires, airplanes.

All reduced to nothingness.
You could never imagine
a sky so expansive, grass

so green, trees so majestic.
A world so peaceful. With the
debris of humanity

expelled from your path, you'll be
swept off your feet by Mother Earth's
omniscient essence. Alight

with the realisation of how
sensationally natural forces
work in harmony with one

another. Not a word spoken.
Not a building in sight. Instantly,
you'll become effortlessly,

fearlessly light. As if the
foundations of body and mind
have slipped away with the crumbling

world. All that remains is your
abundantly pure energy -
swallowing limitless skies

and boundless peripheral
greenery; instinctively
finding grounding in the Earth's core;

basking in unconditional
love, acceptance, togetherness.
Homecoming. Comforted by the

collective certainty of
never again feeling raw nerve
endings of pain. Nor rejection,

self-consciousness, hopelessness,
fear, insecurity, lack.
For you'll always have your own back,

and the universe will always
flow inwardly through your soul,
and outwardly, encompassing

existence. Magnetized. You'll have
no idea of how long the
moment of clarity lasts.

If the curtain fall spans milli-
seconds or days. Whether the
message arrives via the tip

of a lightning bolt, or is
steadily drip-fed like raindrops
from an Amazonian leaf.

Holy water. No date will
be crossed on the calendar,
and boxes around your rebirth

will remain similarly
unchecked. Scrawled memos cast aside -
time markers to which once so

accustomed are now child's play.
Forevermore, simply trust
that you will consider the past

version of yourself a shadow
puppet. A sleepwalker of life,
aimlessly wandering with

unfulfillment to every step.
Existing instead of living.
After awakening it will

become abundantly clear
that your functional mind was
limited to the confines

of your own being. Big fish:
little pond. Once the bank breaks
to reveal infinite ocean,

the fish - having never seen
such expanse before - will be awe-
inspired, and given time to

acclimatise to its new
unchartered environment,
will become illuminated

and will grow to know truth: true
freedom, true happiness, true
appreciation. Through strength of

metabolic enlightenment,
the fish will metamorphosize
into a great wonderland whale,

that can never again be a fish,
for it has justly outgrown the
pond - its past life confined to

five second memory.

COLOURBLIND

Collective conditioning renders
every human colourblind,
since the spectrum of colour
is unique to the eye of the beholder.

Is the dress blue or grey?
Social commentary scrolls
become magician cape insights
into dropped stitches of the matrix.

In infancy, we are taught that *this* hue -
bouncing from source, journeying through
light, finding logic in our brain -
is called red, yellow, pink, or green.

So we come to know the colour
by its assigned name,
which eradicates any space
for individual perception.

Red could paint as yellow in one eye,
pink in the next, but the colour
is assigned the same name
by unnegotiable optical doctrine.

There is no going over the lines
when colouring the world's rainbow.
And so, we will never truly know
what other people see -

what any other person on Earth sees.
Love is a lot like this.
And it is through the prism of love,
we learn to embrace the light.

INTO THE SKID

Enlightenment is her reward for
achieving balance within herself.

In one finger-click, core energies
balance within and pulse permeate

the atoms of her environment.
A single, central entity in

a painting of picturesque nature,
smudges through the canvas, hues bleeding

into one. All defining features
and outlines merge into a dreamlike,

spectacular, technicolour state.
She surrenders totally to the

unknown. Relinquishes control of
the colour wheel of her life. Having

lost all faith in self-navigation,
she turns into the skid of brush strokes

unchartered. An inner frequency
harmonic with Earth's elementary

hum emanates from her physical
membrane. Peace.

LONELY HIKER

Oh, the sadness.
The realisation that the path-forger
must embark on the journey alone.
Clearing overgrowth of old belief systems
and laying foundations for the new world.
Consciousness amongst unconsciousness.
One giant leap into the unknown.
Guided solely by intuition.
Lonely hiker of oneness.

THROUGH DARKNESS

Through a funny dream
I wake myself laughing -
true belly laughs -
and I realise it's still there.

The alchemy of sadness into laughter
at the core of my existence.
The will to make life light
always within me.

If only in my dreams
for now.
Joy!
The path I'm supposed to walk.

I cry for experiencing lightness
I never thought I'd feel again,
drowsily marvel at the complexities
of the human experience.

Then I laugh myself back to sleep
at the ridiculousness of it all;
the fragility of divinity's sleep mask.
It's a funny old game.

CONFLICT CHORDS

Achieving peace requires the bridging
of masculine and feminine poles
within. As with the universal
energies keeping Mother Earth
balancing on her axis, the
human body is alive with
transcendent polarities. When an
individual achieves internal
equilibrium of male and female
polarities, source frequency
effortlessly extends outward -
attuning the collective choir
to the rhythm of truth, climbing note
by note to the eradication
of enduring gender conflict.

THE PATH OF TRUTH

You can't fake loving
yourself, or being
a bearer of light.
The universe sees
past all illusions.
Through its currency
of pure, boundless love,
you will be rewarded
for making decisions
aligning with the
vibration of truth.
As is the tune of
source and soul. Inner
demons, worldly demons
will not lead you home
but towards lust, greed,
manipulation, pride,
deception, power.
A never-ending loop
of suffering, void of
tunnel-end-flickers.
Chose divine surrender
over dancing with
ego ghosts locked within.
Live your life mindfully,
reassemble from scratch,
honour soul purpose.
Only then is there hope
of salvation from
mistruths, fear and lack -
by mirroring light
resounding from the

double-edged dagger
of mortal free will.
A strenuous path,
requiring valour,
expelling those rooted
in eternal darkness,
without insight or strength
to conquer sacred tests
gifted to you from
united consciousness
of our omniscient
cosmos – so it was
preordained that you
would break away from
shackles of molten red
and soar towards violet
flames of serenity.

THE HAPPY KIND

People aren't kind because they're happy,
they're happy because they're kind.
Nothing brings greater peace
than a clear conscience.

ZERO EXERTION

It takes no energy to be authentic.
Soul-synchronised words and actions
flow through human essence
like vapour from warm river rapids.

Authentic energy takes care of itself;
existing without exertion -
eternal abundance the reward
for unconditioned resonance.

Subscribing to masks, illusions
and gameplay is an exhaustive
path of dissatisfaction
and dead ends.

Egoic determination to control
the path of happiness only
complicates and delays the pursuit.
Burnout.

Master code concealment -
the complete library of ethereal
wisdom is encapsulated within
the frequency of authenticity.

Enzymic, magnetizing. Atoning
tide to shore, sunflower to sun, leaves
to wings to hearts. Vitalizing newborn
lungs with pure organic charge.

The beating kiss of life. A language
long forgotten by disconnected beings,
deafly unconscious to the cries
of Mother Earth, at the demise

of her mother tongue. Near extinction,
at the sole mercy of surrendered souls
to champion her charge towards
authentic grace. Illuminated.

HATE SPACE

Self-hatred festers
in the space between
authenticity
and masked persona.

The further we stray
from sacred purpose,
the more ardently
we scorn the journey.

STAGE DOOR

We are each cast on Earth to play our part.
This dense incarnation, where conformity
imprisons the masses, sucking oxygen
from the atmosphere like a gas chamber.

Titanium walls depriving humans
of free will, keeping us locked in fear.
We're easier to herd when we're afraid.
Easier to manipulate when our

frequency is reduced to that of the
limiting belief systems we serve.
Pay your taxes. Climb the ladder of
someone else's dream. Retire with more cash

than you ever had, in the nick of
fatal time, and call it a life well lived.
Stay exactly where you are. Ignore your
soul's cry for something greater, something real.

There must be more than this. Stay. Stay for
the kids, stay for the money, stay out of fear.
Fear will keep you trapped anyway; the greatest
weapon against mankind. And the clincher is

that's it's all an illusion. Fear is simply
negative thought, and thoughts do not exist.
They are not tangible in any form,
in any timeline. Passing clouds of 'what if'?

To surpass fear, you must transcend the ego,
for at your core lies authenticity.
An excruciating feat when we've been
conditioned by a culture submerged in

inauthenticity. Competitiveness,
lying and manipulation poster
children for progress. Personal happiness
above collective happiness. Self-serving

love above unconditional. Oneness
massacred by men in high places.
We are great pretenders, having settled
into our parts so well that we now

mirror our superficial reality.
We ourselves are the illusion. One by one
we must remove our masks and exit through
the stage door. Beyond which there is light.

CHANGE IS CONSISTENCY

Life isn't challenging,
it's faith-inducing.

You may not love every minute,
but you can find love in every minute.

Challenges are catalysts for change,
and change is the consistency of the universe.

Resisting change is like winter avalanching spring,
it will only lead to suffering.

You must surrender and evolve,
to reap the summer harvest.

WOMAN LASSOS UNIVERSE

You need not give me
the universe -
I found it for myself,
within myself.

There is nothing you
can provide for me
that is not amply
balanced within me.

But you may sit beside me.
No past, no future. Just
stargazing in the moment,
grounded by flight.

THE ASSIGNMENT

Never hate yourself for loving,
for daring to love is not for the weak.
That your love was misdirected,

unreciprocated or abused
has nothing to do with you. Change
the narrative that you are naïve

for trying to understand love -
it is the purpose of our existence.
Some are simply not strong enough

to honour the assignment. They may lie,
cheat, manipulate their way to a pass,
but it's entirely superficial

in the end; all meaning lost once
the ink dries. This is destiny work -
the universe has no time for

illusions. Carried on the wind,
she whispers her secret. Grab a pen,
are you ready? 'Love yourself first'.

CARCINOGENIC

Narcissism is cancer
of consciousness: one rogue cell's
toxic metamorphosis,
steely grey against the grain,
contaminating every
healthy sphere on its path of
destruction. Self-awareness
disabled, until a mass
of darkness suffocates the
nucleus of saintly spores.
All light extinguished. Forget
soul purpose - existence is
fight or flight now. Confusion,
panic, anger. Tormented
thoughts, silent screams of a doomed
system hijacked. Even when
the battle's over, evil
piously purged from benumbed
flesh, the clinical curtain
of illusion stoically
drawn, romanticism will
sometimes crawl back to foggy
scenes, seeking a confession,
a trace of humanity
from the enemy, who once
nurtured neck-noose mutations
of love with Hyde eyes twinkling.
Narcissism is caustic,
advantageous, nihilistic,
crazed, engulfing, relentless.
It is you.

SHARING SPACE

There was a time
I shared space
with true emptiness.

Made endless allowances,
hopped on hot coals,
bled my inner light

for an entity whose mood
depended solely
on external factors:

how full its stomach,
how stroked its ego,
how smashing its sale.

The variables of daily life
dictating every output
without cognitive awareness.

Knee jerk reactions,
limbs flying everywhere,
volume jarred to the max.

Battery reset out of reach,
control, alt, deleting
my presence to survive.

Never an authentic smile,
every moment resounding
from titanium walls.

Happiness a display,
never a feeling.
Snap shots for morale

of ghostly absent moments.
The exorcism
of this non-existence

imparted an inner assurance
that I need never drain others
simply to exist.

For my happiness is born
from divinely planted seeds
within my soul.

And on this borrowed time
I vow to share space
only with light.

PLODDING AROUND

He doesn't know
what she's moaning about;
all she does all day
is plod around.

School runs, nappies, laundry,
groundhog cartoon animals,
snotty noses, soggy reading records.
They don't want their kids in daycare.

Give him half an hour when he gets in,
he works full-time, remember.
Paid labour, therefore gospel.
Untouchable dystopian hero.

With aggression as his weapon
he'll coerce dialogue so that
their dynamics meet his every need,
gifting his handmaid bedtime.

Of course, he'll call incessantly,
giving the illusion of connection.
Then crawl home to sleep, scowl wiped clean
for his positive reinforcement puppet.

Now, he orbits her rejuvenated glow
behind white-picket boundaries of her creation,
as he burrows and sweats, floppy haired,
coaxing children in his charge.

She peacefully sighs, observing
the beauty of universal justice.
Long non-linear years, every intent absorbed.
Plodding looks messy on him.

C*NT FLOWERS

Hannah thinks it's ridiculous
you get offended
when I call you a c*nt.

She can't believe how sensitive
you are - she and her boyfriend
say it all the time.

Lighten up. Goodwill flowers
to brighten the kitchen,
heart of the home.

A watercolour few weeks
of romantic renaissance
until hateful red splatters

of blasphemous pesticides
witlessly settle upon
wilting clover leaves.

Toxic photosynthesis.
Our secret botanical
abuse cycle.

TRUE HATE'S LOVE

She naively thought
the decision to leave
would be the hard part.

She could never have anticipated
the destruction of the storm
in the wake of waking up.

The walls of his empire
entirely dependent
on disordered conformism.

Left foot - right foot.
Yes Sir - no Sir.
Keep in line.

Then, above tired bell ringing
and trauma patched with tape
he told her he respected her bravery.

A handshake in the ring
of a fight never meant
for her.

DRAMA QUEEN

When my therapist said,
grey rock: no contact,
it sounded comically extreme:
I'm no drama queen.

It fell through my thoughts
like breeze through leaves.
Never taking root in my neurones,
tangled as they were.

I can handle my narcissist,
he's only half bad, after all.
Jekyll and Hyde, redeeming qualities,
a hurt little boy deep down.

Why does she keep calling him my abuser?
Her sympathetic eyes make me recoil.
I feel like I'm lying for attention.
'Get over yourself', I hear him say.

I fiddle with my rings.
Now I'm in the victim's seat.
She's misunderstood the situation.
Doesn't she realise how strong I am?

I'm mother supreme:
phoenix rising. Powerful
by design, wilful by nature.
Wilful ignorance.

Time heals everything:
what once were textbook words
are now ethical footprints.
My greatest soul lesson.

I'm forever divinely altered, aligned.
His detachment from the whole
magnetised me to its core.
An enduring lesson in balance -

but balance, nonetheless.
Goodbye shadow dweller,
I belong to the scattered rays
of sunbeam haze.

MY PART

I still hear your voice sometimes,
did you know that?
I anticipate your answer
right after my words are released.

My omniscient perspective
of your narcissistic wirings
means I anticipate your next move,
as if you come with a manual.

You were there in therapy, too.
Your voice always countering mine;
your gaslighting so engrained in my psyche
that scripted lines shadowed my every word.

I felt I was lying. Being dramatic.
In the early weeks, I was preoccupied with
'But this is only my side of the story',
'How do you know I'm telling the truth'?

Narcissistic abuse runs deep.
You altered my version of reality,
and my soul's blueprint is strong,
pure, fun. It was not yours to contort.

The pendulum had to swing so far skyward
that the toxic chain around my neck snapped,
untethering me from your control,
once and for all.

I had to perceive you as inhuman
to regain my own humanity.
It had to happen
this way.

That's how we must coexist now.
Actions have consequences,
and my euphoric peace is justification
that this new equilibrium must prevail.

Maybe one day I'll catch a glimpse
of inner peace in your eye and smile,
imagining you beside your inner child
on a seaside bench, making amends.

Ever mindful that even the hypothetical
start of your journey of realignment
must never cross-contaminate
with that of my healed womanhood.

Cosmically shielded from your aura.
Visions from a parallel vortex.
From my safe space, I will hold space
for your salvation.

UNTETHERED

Existing
without
attachment

is exemption
from
manipulation.

NOW SHOWING

The problem with broken loyalty
is that you can wholeheartedly forgive -
release all remnants of resentment,
leave the pain in the past
and forge forward in the present.

However, the snag in the loop endures.
Time rotates with resistance, since wounds
of the heart are not confined to memory
time capsules, chronologically stored
in cognitive archive.

Affixing a label reading 'past'
to grainy film reel cannot
possibly conceal the infiniteness
of betrayal once the scene
is projected.

Just as love transcends timelines,
a meteoric gulf now exists
in every timeline of the union.
The frequency of the connection
permanently lowered.

Once destruction penetrates
the wider consciousness,
dim the lights, reduce the sound,
only a matter of time
until curtains close.

SIT WITH HER

Is there any man capable of just sitting with a woman?
Acknowledging, revering and protecting her power.
Yet being confident enough to sit peacefully and share
her energetic space. Why must this be fantasy?

Wounded man, regardless of how pure his soul's intention,
automatically seeks weakened spirit when connecting with
an authentic woman. Ammunition for when her self-assurance
becomes threatening. A back-pocket tool for devaluation.

The tragic paradox is that her authenticity is what he likes
about her. Loves, even. However, with no sacral desire stronger
than a threat to his ego, he resorts to mindless attacks
on her emotional triggers, stab after stab -

when her assured existence illuminate his insecurities.
His pride is paramount. An injured lion, encaged by limiting
social paradigms that block the expansion of his heart,
mind and soul. Pack mentality. Survival.

And so, he loses this one. And the next. Gazing with forlorn fury
from the thorned veil of his own creation. Powerless to see
past the illusion. Eternally regretful, but lacking the insight
and strength to change.

He competed with soul that called for mirroring,
and in doing so sabotaged a pure connection.
It's all murky water now. She only ever asked for him
to sit with her.

HALF LIGHT

There are those among us
who are neither here nor there,
existing in a swirling
sandstorm between divine
polarities. Dreaming
of light without the courage
to break free from the shackles
of sallow shadow ego.
Hope lies within the fact
self-serving tendencies can
be realised. Fierce existence -
where none is born pure: bias,
malice, jealousy, anger
within us all. The beauty
of this journey is that
it's never too late for
lost souls to be guided back
to the path of light. Though,
this transition requires
tremendous self-awareness
and strength. Culling the ego,
starting fresh, a suicide
of sorts. Unfiltered love -
sprouting from the depths of
conscious thought, channelling
through pulsating mind portals,
igniting synergetic
chakra fields in the body.
Consciousness is the gateway
to the soul: to be fully
conscious is to be fully
source-aligned. Thus, to achieve

genuine salvation,
there must be capacity
for cursive soul connection.
Crushingly, society's
relentless encouragement
of attachment to selfish
commodity means many
are destined for a life
of eternal sleepwalking.

SELF-PROCLAIMED

You can call yourself an empath
to every pair of fresh, eager ears,
but if you're only empathetic
towards people from whom you have
something to gain: those who validate,
supply or serve you in some way -
yet to others are indifferent,
volatile or spiteful - you're simply
an emotional broker. A true
empath is seamlessly kind to all.

PLAYER

The player will spend a lifetime
chasing illusory goals to
be the first, have the most, do it best -
reign supreme in a dystopian
leaderboard rooted in fear and lack.
The higher they progress in their low
vibrational arena, the more
distracted they become from the
true goal of returning to source.
As they trip over their own feet,
collecting plastic medals for
superficial validation,
say nothing. You are not in the same
stadium, let alone on the same
circuit. Sit peacefully in your court
where there are no stop-clocks, spectators,
beaten tracks. For competitiveness
cannot exist in a life of
blissful, ethereal stasis.

TRY ME

She who
rejects ego,
embodies divine love,
introspects with intent,
resides below superficiality,
loves herself unconditionally,
balances emboldened feminine essence -
with healed masculine energy,
moves in soul-alignment,
has unwavering morals,
speaks with integrity,
serves the whole,
fights injustice,

will always be too much
for a wounded man.

LOST SOULS

So dependent on control, they can never love.
So incapable of self-awareness, they can never evolve.
So entrenched in toxicity, they can never resolve karma.
So hostile to community, they can never serve the collective.
So terrified of digesting emotions, they spit their pain on others.
So void of internal affirmation, they feast on external validation.
So intrinsically self-serving, they are ignorant to altruism.
So chronically self-loathing, they target the self-assured.
So superficial, connection to soul is futile.
Every lifeline thrown to humanity
from the universe - forever out of reach.
Ascension impossible for those at the burning red
of the virtue spectrum, polar-opposing the violet torch
of unconditional love, with total lack of goodness. Lost ethos.
Unity consciousness verses separation consciousness.
Ultimate connection verses ultimate disconnect.
High vibration verses low vibration.
Light verses dark.

THE EGO OF YANG

We both know what it was, though neither
of us acknowledged it: I was too strong for you.
You couldn't meet me there, so you ran.

But you didn't run authentically, gracefully or gently.
You ran by breaking me. Weaponizing my insecurities.
Using my deepest trauma as a shield for yours.

And I forgave you, because my language is soul
connection, and seeing the potential of yours,
I naively believed you'd magnetise towards growth.

So blinded by wilful ignorance, I forgave you
endlessly, every time you returned, thinking you
were healed enough to match my light.

Buckling beneath it when you fell short. Casting
me out, before I exposed you. Your inauthenticity,
your false persona, your ego fort.

Balancing on fragile twigs, collected from
your dreamworld jungle. Who are you?
You became your worst nightmare;

a green-eyed dream-state monster.
Mystics said your soul mirrored mine -
to hell it did! My soul rejects ego.

So I wear the skulls around my neck, as I continue
the mission alone, a single flame dancing in the name
of truth and genuine love.

Your gypsy sky dweller, flighty for all but the egoless.
You visit my dreams less now - sometimes a devil
in the mirror, your knife in my back, jolting me awake.

Other times, walking towards the beach,
where fireworks adorn the shoreline. Glancing
back as if I'm a stranger. Enchanted no more.

HEYOKA EMPATH

A soul connection
is good to no one
if ego attachment
blocks peace and lowers
vibrations on blessed soil.

The whole thing becomes
paradoxical.
She would have loved you
unconditionally.
You knew - that's what scared you.

So accustomed to
fearing the real you
was unlovable
at molten-core level.
So you blocked her. Hardened

defence, bordering
on attack. Building
ego characters
so familiar
that the distinction

between truth and facade
was blurred. Sabotaging
the union became
militant reflex;
her devaluation

an easy target.
Collateral damage.
You desired her
insecure like you.
Festering imbalance.

Divinely shielded from
manipulation and
mistruths, her Dakini
power had you by
the throat. Backed into

naked shadow corners;
your escape puny,
predictable. Teenage
gameplay on middle-aged
time.

KARMIC CATALYSTS

It's not that they don't have souls,
it's just that theirs are so neglected
and minimally evolved

that they are fundamentally estranged
from their higher selves.
Less personality disorder: more soul disorder.

Tragedy in abundance - since
monumental metaphysical plans
were never destined for them.

In this incarnation,
their mission is to guide soul ties
into realising what love is not -

the wounds they inflict
triggering intense growth
in their recipients, the healers.

Their heists of noir
elevating energetic frequency
of lightworkers,

pushing them
into the blissful realm
of infinite love.

When bodies expire and souls transcend,
theirs will arrive at the stage
of development achieved on Earth:

chaotic and needy,
trapped in perpetual
loops of childhood.

Whereas the souls of empaths,
wise as ancient willows, will bask
in the sunset of fulfilled lives.

Perhaps the saddest part
of releasing soul misalignments
is the realisation that

so absolute is the generational full stop,
so disparate the polarising evolution,
so guttering the lesson

that soul pairings of such ordained
fatality likely won't occur again
in any other lifetime.

The aftermath air of wildfire anarchy
whispers confirmation
of their single union. Their finite hour.

So, be grateful for those who transformed
love into power, trust into manipulation,
loyalty into dependency.

They knew no better.
Embrace the pain they inflicted,
in the knowledge

that it was all part
of the bigger picture -
of your soul's evolution.

Your awakening. Bringing you closer
to the most authentic version of you,
in all your transcendent glory.

Karmic catalyst;
from your darkness
comes light.

EGO BREAK

The weak use ego
to break the soul.

The strong use soul
to break the ego.

SQUANDERED RICHES

There are those who abuse love: lost causes.
Fundamentally unable. Deficient.
But by far the most tragic
are missed opportunities of love
from the able.

Those who have the potential to love purely,
but squander their riches for ego's gain.
So tormented by lack from the unconscious,
that when faced with genuine love,
they simply do not recognise it -

remaining stagnant, apathetic, sabotaging, running -
and subsequently missing their window of light.
Fear as their ally, they would rather let the opportunity go
than dare to embrace something so monumentally
vulnerable and unknown.

Terrified to expose their true persona, raw nerves
at the core. It's a blessing that regret only lasts
a lifetime, with remorse relinquishing in ashes to ashes
and matrix minds watering down the intensity of eternal
soul longing.

You'll get another chance. The universe is forgiving.
In the next life, when you return, shed a layer of armour.
Lower your shield low enough to look your divine in the eye,
and embrace the mirror-self reflected back to you
through her crystal lens.

Witness your boyhood sigh in surrender.
It's been a long journey,
you've walked through fire,
you're tired. In the next one,
come home.

BOUND

Even when
you don't love me,
you're at your worst,
you hide your true self,
you take without returning,
you're threatened by my power,
your exile is the best outcome,
you sabotage every sentiment,
you run and run again,
you succumb to fear.
Even then.

EMPOWERED

A wounded man has no idea what to do with a woman in her power:
a woman who is emotionally, mentally and financially secure.

He will sound her out to find her vulnerability. Something to grab onto.
In the hope of lowering her vibration. To reduce her to a frequency

similar to his - that of lack - on which to lay the fibreglass
foundations of co-dependency.

To his fury, he will instantly hit a wall with an emboldened woman,
since she intuitively rejects attachment, seeking only

balanced connection, ever respectful of her righteous
relationship with her inner self and the cosmos.

Devaluing her won't work. Jealousy gambles won't work.
Superficial offerings won't work. Social contracts won't work.

Wounded men and women alike are polluted in their approach
to establishing and maintaining genuine, loving connections.

Partnerships in which both parties are emotionally whole -
consequently sharing this wholeness with the other,

and receiving wholeness in return:
pure unity, complete love.

Centuries of bowing to toxic social paradigms and beliefs
has resulted in generations of fatally wounded

masculine and feminine energies - ultimately forging
a race resistant to surrendering to equal union

and love without limitation. Love emanating from
untethered souls, as opposed to ego.

Illusory love has become normalised, with its web
of conditions, control and dependency.

A healed man will find a woman in her power and walk beside her.
Guarding her Goddess energy to ensure she flourishes in her power.

Protector of wisdom, provider of stable foundations, leader of logic.
The bones of an empowered man. Where is he?

HANGMAN

Healthy love is not
controlling someone
into treating you how
you want to be treated.

It is giving someone
the complete freedom
to approach you as
they freely desire.

Only then will their
true, unabridged nature
be revealed. Graciously
hand them the loosest rope.

If they hang themselves,
it is clear suicide
and you're spared enmeshment
with their weak morals.

Allow a person to
do what they want to do,
for this exposes
what they would rather do.

CATALYST

The malevolent are lost
causes in this existence.
They will have another
chance in the next. Here, now,
they serve to spark the soulful
into awakening.
To strike-illuminate
the sacral meaning of love,
by demonstrating what love
is indisputably not.
Correctness born of mistakes;
lessons born of the journey;
enlightenment born of the
catalytic path to peace.

GOODNIGHT, GEMSTONE

And so, you were gifted one of the rarest gems on the planet.
Illuminating hues that were completely alien to you; prisms of light
so intense that you felt unworthy of holding them in your hands.

You were accustomed to pebbles. You knew how to handle pebbles -
a playful grip, then skimmed over the ocean and back to shore to seek
the next thrill. You weren't expecting this once-in-a-lifetime find.

This magnetic missing piece of the universe. You instantly recognised
that its purity had the potential to expose long-supressed shadows
and blindly slice through illusions.

Intuitively, you knew that embracing this rarity would require a vast
shift in existence, fine-tuning of perspective and major heart expansion.
Ultimately, you were too scared to wholeheartedly face it.

So you hesitated. And the universe held its breath, releasing an audible
sigh, carried on dovetail feathers, when you once again returned
to your mound of pebbles. What a way to devalue a gemstone.

As blood-orange meteor-rays melted into the ocean and divine justice rose
from foamy embers, your back-pocket treasure began to lose its shine.
For no distance can outrun karma; no jungle thicket can escape judgement.

The sky was dark with disappointment by the time you made your decision.
Brimming with delayed Emperor vision, you reached into your pocket
to claim your prize, failing to realise that universal law holds the final judgmen

In place of Empress encapsulated, you withdrew the fool card. The consequen
of approaching divine femininity with gameplay. Serendipitous misalignment,
perhaps. Or the fatal lap of a lion too afraid escape the mind's enclosure.

Lick your wounds in peace. Return with less bravado in the next. Paradise. Where your gemstone will shine brighter, ascend faster, cut sharper. As if chiselled by Jupiter's knife. Head to firework shores. Start over.

HOPE

I hope your sky radiates enlightenment
and your moon shares her sleep secrets.

I hope your thoughts are serenely steady
like the waves you atone with.

I hope you've escaped the karmic wheel
and discovered your self-worth.

I hope you've found the peace you were seeking
that you willed to source through me.

I hope your mythical dream lurkers have ceased
and your ears awakened to the siren-call of swifts.

I hope this released contract brings eternal comfort
and your ascension is smooth and empowering.

This I hope for you.

UNIVERSAL ERROR

There's been a huge mistake,
I'm not supposed to be here.
Not for a second -
not even on a visa.

THE OTHER

For some, love is a vehicle
of control through which
needs of the self are met:

personal ego validated,
personal emotions regulated,
personal scarcity substantiated.

Very little is about the other.
They are simply a power supply
of enduring light

in an otherwise dark space -
momentarily vital
but ultimately replaceable.

A mutual meeting of needs
is essential
for harmonious union.

But still, love goes beyond this -
love is a genuine quest to fulfil
the happiness of the other.

If relational unhappiness is voiced
and met with lack of empathy,
lack of behavioural adjustment

and lack of genuine, lasting action,
then this is not love.
This is arrogant assurance

in the power of emotional ties
and wilful disbelief that the other
will ever leave.

CO-DEPENDENCY

Insecurity leads people to form attachments
as opposed to connections
with people and their surroundings.

This idea is nothing new - fundamental ideology
of paramount religions. The lack of unconditional love
within oneself causes an internal imbalance of polarities.

Yin: yang. Shiva: shakti. Feminine: masculine.
Such energies can only osmose with atmospheric frequency
if concentrations are equal on both sides of the membrane.

Perhaps biology plays a part in mankind's
predisposition to interpersonal dependency;
human young are highly dependent on caregivers,

which results in intense attachments being forged
early in infancy. The optimal 'just right' balance
between emotional and physical nurturing is tentative:

a child should receive ample demonstrations of healthy,
genuine love, for mental soundness - in conjunction with
integral co-dependent habits, for lifelong biological fulfilment.

This is where the paradox lies. The survival
of human infants depends on exhaustive attachment,
whereas the essence of existence is connection.

Both are infused into our DNA - therefore play out
in our adult relationships and lifestyles.
Potentially to encourage a tower moment,

in which the two meet one another in meteoric collision -
the desired outcome being the realisation that
attachment-driven lives are the downfall of humanity.

Ancient Taoist philosopher Lao-Tzu had the notion
that the ideal state of existence is,
'connected to everything but attached to nothing'.

Arguably idealistic in our echoing societal chamber;
whereby money is essential for survival,
superficiality promoted and external validation normalised.

Perhaps the ultimate solution is to coexist
within the polarities, finding a sweet spot
between the gulfs of loving association.

LOVE IS ABSENCE

Genuine love is when contributing to your partner's peace
is of equal importance to having your own needs met.

Often, when attachment styles differ, triggered wounds attack -
coaxing compliance to self-serving terms and conditions,

at the expense of disrupting the peace of the other.
This is not love. True love is self-soothing unconscious fears

for the wellbeing of the relationship. A blank canvas waiting
for collaborative creation of harmony and trust.

Love is surrendering. Resetting conditioned
beliefs, nervous systems and patterns.

Love is absence of the impulse
to control, change or restrict the other.

Dependency and love are opposing forces: the greater
the dependency, the more starved the lifeforce of love.

POLYSTYRENE WALLS

When you partner with someone
heavily in ego mindset
the entire foundation of your union
will be dependent on ego.

Since egocentric morality
gravitates towards fear, lack
and illusion, so too will
their free-will choices.

Together, the strongest creation
you can hope for
is a co-dependent house
made from polystyrene walls.

When you partner with
a soul-atoned spark,
the cornerstone of every decision
will be grounded in integrity.

The partnership will provide
consistent, authentic grounding
from which to build reality.
Brick by loving brick.

DETHRONING EGO

Don't allow ego to enthrone your thoughts;
operate predominantly through the observing mind.
That is, the space that perceives thought.

The thinking mind is a stubborn machine of conformity,
worry, logic, judgment. It is an unforgiving
stream-of-consciousness steeped in matrix mentality.

By contrast, the observing mind is a calm, conscious
bystander to the processes of unbounded thought -
monitoring and regulating its behaviour.

It is the cognitive home for self-awareness; mediating
overreactions, rationalising spiralling thought
and soothing panic.

Through cognitive training, observing perspective
has the capacity to wholly overthrow thinking perspective,
replacing it with a temporary nirvana of stillness.

Hierarchal thoughts, created by persona and attached
to your identity, are not you. The essence of you is what remains
in the absence of thought. In your pure, unequivocal presence.

CONTRACTUAL

A parent does not look into their newborn daughter's eyes
and think, 'I will open my heart to you, based on conditions':
That you are beautiful. That you are tolerant. That you are receptive.

Nor would they meet their son's gaze with similar obligations
for love: That you are handsome. That you are successful.
That you provide.

Deep love is formed effortlessly with our children, because the bond
is not hinged on diplomacy. It's not about what our children
'bring to the table', nor how the relationship benefits us.

We enter into the connection aware that our devout adoration
will never be matched. Yet somehow, we find comfort in this.
It is unattached, selfless love in its purest form.

What if we were to approach our romantic relationships
with the same gusto as our parental offerings? That is to extend
genuine love, without the scaffolding of superficial conditions.

To completely shed the limiting, engendered social beliefs
that have imprinted on our nervous systems. How would romance
look beyond surface-level lenses? Two silent spirits and no noise.

Maybe we've achieved harmonious partnerships in ethereal playgrounds,
and that's why our souls crush during heartbreak. It's not supposed
to be this way. Maybe we're all just one incarnation away,

with the energy conserved solely for our children in this timeline.
Those bright-eyed star seeds, who breathe hope into the trials of love.
Maybe our purpose in this lifetime is to simply learn from them.

PEACE PARADOX

We are taught to love thy neighbour,
without exception,
because we are all one.

What about soul hijackers?
Spiritual blocks?
Abusers?

As the scripture goes,
once karmic contracts are completed,
and lessons in 'un-loving' realised

noxious counterparts will fade
from benevolent lives
indefinitely.

However, sometimes
confused brain chemicals
remain attached to toxic love.

Fear must be eradicated to release the bond,
because to love malevolence is to validate
injustice - glucose for gluttonous darkness.

It is to exist in the past -
a place of illness and suffering.
A constant backwards glance to trauma.

It is to leave the basement door ajar,
so manipulative cries from below
can always be heard.

To remain lovingly attached
is a sign of enduring
trauma bonding.

Tethered to low vibrational cycles,
unwittingly surrendering gracious souls
to energy vampires.

Personal boundaries must be reclaimed;
the source blotted out and all paperwork
thrown to the flames.

The Great Peace Paradox is that
we are not obligated to love
those who obliterate our light.

Doing so will prevent the ascension towards
unconditional love. Nor should we hate, since
this weighs just as heavy on the conscience.

Instead, we should naturally settle
at a place of neutrality
and apathy.

Practicing gratitude for their role
in the collective evolution -
merciless portals to peace -

whilst realising that emotional peddling
need not continue after the
completion of the karmic cycle.

Surplus emotional investment
would be to defy
divine intervention.

Illusions of love are temporary
by cosmic design; preparation for
unmasked eyes that feel like home.

EMPATHS BE LIKE

Only a true, ridiculous empath
would feel guilty for the financial cost
of the love-bombing stage - to the extent
that they'd consider breaking no contact
to offer to contribute towards their
own emotional manipulation.
This is why the universe loves empaths.

WHEREIN LIES THE TOXICITY?

Masculine and feminine energies exist inside
every human being. Neither accumulated
nor regenerated, they are accessible to all.

It is the duty of the individual to raise their vibration
to activate these polarities and alchemise them
into balance. Therein lies harmony.

Women often grasp this concept with tender excitement;
fully prepared to embrace the divine masculine
within them, as part of them.

Whereas men tend to approach the notion with a tight fist.
Emasculated. Offended. How can someone advocate
for an entity they're afraid of?

Not his fault, rather the effect of social conditioning.
Not until gender equality is the collective objective
of all humanity - will peace prevail.

First and foremost, men must surrender to the fear
of the emboldened feminine, both as an external energy
and a facet of their own identity.

INHALE: EXHALE

Neither women nor men have it easy.
As the walls of this social paradigm close in,

women build the strength to release
centuries of invalidated emotions,

while men build the strength
to feel them.

An inhale: exhale
of stagnant vitality.

Source energy is purest at the mountain peak,
where male dominance waves his flag.

She has a treacherous climb
before she can echo into the abyss,

while he has hierarchal freedom
at the tip of his nose -

he simply has to take a breath
and surrender.

The feminine quest to regain power
from a centuries-old belief system

is no less difficult than the masculine quest
to relinquish power.

Fear of change overshadows both entities,
with resistance to vulnerability at the root.

It takes strength to be strong,
just as it takes strength to be vulnerable

Neither women nor men
have it easy.

DARK ERA

The nineteenth-century was a nonsensical time for women
in the West. Invisible portraits on a social wall that was
economising, industrialising and developing. Without her.

Mothers would conceive, carry and nurture male infants,
in the branded awareness that birth would mark a tectonic
power shift between the two. Before the cutting of cords,

her son would be her superior. Heir to masculine ancestral lineage.
Eligible forger and money spinner. Destined to access
worldly delights forever out of reach for her.

If at any point she would become maddened by the mundanity
of her limited existence, he would have the authority
to consider her hysterical - institutionalise her, perhaps,

to receive treatment for what his kindred society broke.
Not that bearing a daughter would be a sweeter pill to swallow.
This paradoxical duty would weigh equally as heavy -

that of adoringly shaping a passionate feminine energy,
expecting every trace to vanish in the dust of childhood -
in the wake of her life sentence as social spectator.

Cordially, an equalising force is charging the hemisphere
of Eden. Propelled by the scales of justice and cosmic
intervention: the empowered feminine is rising.

Now it's soul warfare. Modern women have been granted a
ballot ticket to occupy the same space as men. Thinking, speaking
and acting as men. But not without opposition.

Now mothers raise sons and daughters at war with one another.
Despite blueprints of gender equality gradually passing the bar,
many men are resisting the emotional work required to create

harmonious social relations with women. Authenticity,
vulnerability, compassion, empathy and receptivity must be
self-cultivated in order to atone with feminine counterparts.

For generations, such attributes have been innately embraced by women
and suppressed by men, meaning the dusty labour of inner work for the
emotional osmosis of this shift settles largely on shoulders of the masculine.

Mothers must be the guiding light, continuing to teach sons
and daughters alike the healing power of gender wholeness. This time,
there must be no social deprivation on either side.

BALL AND CHAIN

The differentiating factor
between marriage and romantic bonds
is legal or religious paper.

For thousands of years, marriage has been
a fundamental factor in wax
stamping unhealthy relationships;

the sanctity of sacred vows 'til
death a bell jar for bad behaviour.
Thankfully, the landscape is changing.

In the developed world we're living
longer, money is accessible
to all genders and there's more support

for mothers. This evolution is
triggering for insecure manhood,
because for so long wedlock has been

an enabler of lacking social
beliefs, control and conditional
love. Now men must do the inner work,

shed their 'comfort-in-control' mindset
and strike a base-line balance with the
opposite sex: feminine divine.

And the bullish ego is bucking.
The time is up. Integrity and
soul alignment are the new power.

THE TRUTH DIVIDE

A great misconception of society is that the
fundamental dividing factors between human beings
relate to ethnicity, religion, status and power.

Whilst it's undeniable that differing belief systems and lifestyles
forge disparity amongst the whole, there is a greater conflict
at play. One that overshadows ecosystems of social segregation.

This is the universal conflict of authenticity. Authentic existence
means being in alignment with the soul's purpose - a practice
requiring focused introspection and self-awareness.

It is to connect to the sacred source of truth and wisdom. To act
authentically is to behave in alignment with the soul's pure nature.
To speak authentically is to verbalise the soul's pure intention.

Virtuous mindsets are high vibrational - the frequency of genuine love.
Light-emboldened individuals emit an energetic pulse capable
of raising that of the collective,

with a single awakened person yielding the capacity
to activate hundreds, through as little as a passing
brush with their aura of truth.

MR GREY

Online dating - it's all grey.
Solely superficial aspects of human beings
pinned to a conveyor belt of social judgment;
egotism condensed into an app.

First round: look pretty.
Second round: checklist consignment.
Third round: red buzzer swipe.
Illusions, illusions, illusions

A social experiment
of enduring performance
that rarely surpasses
the magic third date.

The only way to meet people
in this age of technology.
Has anyone told destiny -
does she have a password?

Humanity reduced to pixelated mirage.
Shameless self-advocates,
master manipulators,
the catfish that got the cream.

Pick me, pick me!
I'm the best hologram
of my sex, for sex, with the sex
I so desire.

Ignore the fact that we're at war
with one another;
a vicious feminist-misogynist riot
raging beneath each match.

Modern suitor's privileged,
prize-winning quest for partners
in crimes of energy exploitation.
Can I wake up yet?

MAD WORLD

You should be crazy in this world.
If you're not buckling under
the chaos of it all, open your eyes!

Our elemental reality is doomed.
Society spinning on superficiality,
galvanized by likes, money, ego.

Void validation taking us away
from who we are at soul level -
the beating hive of belonging.

The only option is to find a way
to straddle the two: tick by
in the timepiece of illusion,

whilst keeping your head above
water, in survival mode
on a sinking Earth plane.

DESIGNER BAGS

How can it be that you step over
breathing sleeping-bags in designer
doorways, clutching thousand-pound satchels,
without feeling charitable weight?
How can it be that you treat fallen
angels of the collective as if
they are lower than you, because the
numeric bricks of their financial
construct fell, and yours tentatively
remain? Your lives are more akin than
you realise. Both trapped in cycles of
low vibration. Both victims of the
human experience. Of a world
with fractured united empathy.
Their tumble is just more tangible.
Imagine how it could be if you
atoned with one another. If you
alchemised receptive energy
so that validation came not from
peacock ostentation, vanity,
but from filling another's heart with
love and value. Those spectacular,
ludicrous, glamorised containers,
that lose their shine the second they touch
the toilet floor. Consumerism
really got you. Heavy baggage. Light
energy caught in the space between
slumbering breath and long-lasting-lip-
stick, through which crimson whispers to Our
Father slip. Kingdom. Power. Glory.

THIRST TRAP

Strive to see your body subjectively;
a mere avatar in the game of creation.
Recognise that your energy is your authenticity.
To garner power, attention or validation from your appearance
is a deadly trap. Those who become attached to aesthetics
magnetise this energy outwards, thus becoming
a lighthouse for superficial relationships.
Looks fade, love is timeless.

LOTTERY

She always had a contradictory attitude
to playing the lottery. Her participation,
fuelled by the consumerist desire
of 'winning big', is fickle.

Cards of luck instantly burn
holes in her pocket,
and go unchecked
for several days.

Does she really want this?
Would she be fulfilled by a free windful?
Or would she feel thoroughly undeserving,
as if skipping steps?

Her flames of hyper-independence
seek reward for talented workmanship
and yearn to earn worthy abundance -
finding little joy in wanton wealth.

Crucially, does she even want to be rich at all?
Her destiny is to live in quiet harmony with Earth,
at eye level with humanity and nature. Atoning
with the elements, not towering above them.

Money fuels power, control, materialism, conflict.
Currency is the mask of the patriarchy,
concealing sneers of mistrust. She preferred
when notes could be destroyed in the wash.

She'd give half to charity, naturally -
to ease her discomfort, maintain
her vibrational magnetism and keep
her divine contract upstanding.

Don't give her that look, universe.
She already knows her fall from grace
would cause tectonic plates to shudder
between the worlds.

She knows she'll have to keep laser focus;
forever teetering the line tethering dimensions,
hoping not to get sucked into the dark chasm
between illusion and truth.

If she had to choose, she'd abandon everything
for the spiritual. Though she often wonders
how Oprah navigates her filthy rich
journey of enlightenment.

MATRIX MOTHERSHIP

We should all be striving for absolute authenticity.
That is, to show up as soul-aligned versions
of ourselves. Free from ego.

A huge hurdle is that ego and trauma are intertwined.
From infancy and throughout adulthood
exposure to trauma and limiting belief systems

shape the ego, so that we become amalgamated,
foreign personas. Robotic machines programmed
to defend ourselves against repeated attacks.

Sleepwalking, we lose the ability to question the morality
of societal conventions. Nervous systems become
wholly reliant on security from holographic giants.

Like newborns blindly writhing
towards milky scent, we seek validation
from the matrix mothership that feeds us.

Too hungry, thankful, dependent to question the purity
of its nectar gold. This way to validation; trust no one;
wealth is wealth; cities that never sleep.

We feed our fear as opposed to our sanctity -
severed anguishes colliding with one another,
bleeding on those we want to love.

Arouse the subconscious, awaken the slumbering serpent,
return to the self and the whole. Our essence is woven
in purifying love, which our bodies long to channel

and our personas long to honour.
The greatest gift you can give your soul
is a life lived authentically.

KARMIC WHEEL

What if suffering exists because,
since the moment of creation,
humanity has failed to achieve
collective balance. Harmonised energy.

Making suffering not so much a punishment,
rather a byproduct of unresolved energy conflict.
Negative energy offset must go somewhere,
so it seeps into the next timeline. Karma.

This reincarnated force means no evil. It exists
for the purpose of being transformed into light.
We've just never quite got the balance right,
have we? So the cycle continues.

The eternal karmic contract of mankind.
Suffering has a freehold on our existence,
draining our personal and collective peace,
because we are unconscious to the toxic loop.

Trust the divine plan. Surrender
to the universe. Infuse with its energy -
both everything and nothing.
The way out is osmosis.

CHILDHOOD DETACHMENT

The child who responds to caregiver trauma with detachment
is at no advantage to the child who responds with attachment
when it comes to forging healthy connections in adulthood.

However, they will have safter grounding
when relating to the self. Their time alone, isolating,
with stream of consciousness free from control

is a gift - allowing individuals to become comfortable
with their unrefined inner voice. More intuitive;
more assertive; more skilled at self-soothing.

The disadvantage of early detachment with caregivers
is that hyper-independence and disassociation
are common in adulthood.

Free Spirit, Lone Wolf tropes shroud figures
as they mature - undeniably problematic to the self
and the collective, long term.

However, it's easier to coax the mind to embrace connectivity
than to face the monumental task of salvaging self-worth, esteem
and value from the ghostly grasp of generational co-dependency.

GATEKEEPERS OF INNOCENCE

Adults are the gatekeepers of childhood peace.
One such defender is sufficient, since the key
to emotional safety need only rest in one nurturing hand -
though a collaborative handshake is a strengthened workforce.

Gatekeepers sustain the sweetness of the childhood home,
providing a safe environment for young souls
to develop and expand: denying entry to ill intention,
fiercely rejecting dark energy.

Should embroidered vines of trauma stalk the archway,
they will tear the poison from the root.
Gatekeepers need not be parents - they may manifest
as carers, aunts, friends, teachers.

Variable in relationship to the child, though united
in their crucial role as ports of emotional safety.
Those fortunate enough to be entrusted with the trinket box
of infancy must guard it with sacred sovereignty.

For the diminishment of negative forces in youth
ensures sacral energy in adulthood is directed
less towards soul healing, and progressively
towards evolution and expansion.

LUNAR LIFE CYCLE

From birth to death,
humans are conditioned
to accept reality
for what it is.

We accept there is a giant
shape-shifting saucer
in the night sky
without question,

simply because the moon
infiltrates infant belief systems
as a normal facet
of our reality -

a comforting scientific prop
to our daily existence.
The wonder, awe and potentiality
of this planetary phenomena

permanently sucked
from consciousness.
Faithfully blinded to
unquestionable vision.

Only the most curious of minds
will feel the pull to unravel
this black and white
way of thinking.

It is through limitless thought
that the universe
becomes truly limitless
to the individual.

Such curiosity
can be applied
to every detail of life,
including the human body itself.

It's remarkable
to think that the heart -
the organ with cardinal,
anatomical virtue

is simultaneously
capable of feeling
the extremities of
emotional experience.

If we're to consider emotion,
'energy in motion',
does this mean the heart
is the assigned emotional generator?

If so, is emotional energy
carried through blood?
How interwoven are emotions
and cardiology?

Since the human heartrate
accelerates and decelerates
in intrinsic response
to emotions

it would seem there is a prominent
synchronicity between the two.
After all, heartbreak is a viable
cause of death.

ULTRAVIOLET

"The wound is the place that the light enters you". Rumi

It's in her eyes. She will see differently to everyone else.
Watch in wonder as one eye retreats into a cave of darkness,
whilst the other expels the rock to embrace divine lightness.
Tricks of a brain seeking balance.

Her eye is her superpower, never forget that.
Never doubt her. Never look at her with sympathy.
When she finds her voice, hear her out. For every strand
of her soul embodied warrior energy to fight this.

She will never see in 3D. Well, obviously -
she was born to soar above the superficial sphere.
Ethereally contracted for greatness,
this five-dimensional dweller of mine.

ENDURING SEMANTICS

It is captivating to think
of all the words in existence,
we will have a first, and a last.

The most common final word is
'mama', of which some variant
is likely to be the prized first.

Though society may underfund,
misunderstand, confuse, neglect,
ostracise and replace the role

of the mother, it can never
erase Hera's fundamental
footprint on the lifespans she sows.

Her first and purest planted kiss
of unconditional love on
newborn souls enduring until

the end. The most common complete
phrase of the dying: 'I love you'.
The very purpose of human

existence, encapsulated
through familial semantics,
timely exhaled from cherished hearts.

UNEARTHING LOVE

To know love: first place on my list of my hopes for this life.
How naïve of me to think it would be an eureka moment -
a utopian island to be discovered and marked with a flag.
'I've looked love in the eye - and perceive it as such - forevermore'.
I have come to see it as an ever-evolving process;
unearthing soul depths as new lifepath corners are visited.

The teacher who once recited tales of mythical sea creatures,
meandering words carried on contentedness of comforting love,
no longer commits her tone to fantasy after marital deceit.
Her perception of love: hers to his, his to hers, the very notion
of love unexpectedly, permanently chiselled as she nears
her half century of human experience.

Our evolutional dance with love is never final,
so destined are we to perpetually edit, audit and update
our understanding until the day we die - perhaps beyond.
I wonder, when we return home and analyse
our encapsulation of love, will we recoil in disappointment
at how far off the mark we were?

SECRETS

Don't tell anyone our secret -
no one will believe a little girl;
no one will believe a madwoman;
no ballot votes for Miss Irrational.

Throat chakra activated.
Secrets are corrosive to the soul,
and I refuse to be silenced any longer.
Now is the time to speak up.

To light a fire beneath the unconscious,
potent enough to smoke the collective
out of their enduring ego slumber. In the hope
of activating, liberating and inspiring.

Universal timing has activated
my divine consciousness,
divine feminine and divine voice,
at this precise moment, for a reason.

Every fibre of my being
is urging me to run with it.
And so, into the unknown I run,
with unconditional love in my heart.

An abundance of limitless love
greater than any conscious imagining
sits at the peripheral
of our perceived reality.

The messenger's purpose is not to convince others,
but to simply be heard. Therefore, take my words
as they resonate, whilst I spread my wings
and forge a path upwards.

Dwell with me in the sky, if so inclined,
or simply listen to my birdsong in grounded
serenity. But never forget to look up.
It's where the light is.

www.ingramcontent.com/pod-product-compliance
Lightning Source LLC
LaVergne TN
LVHW051648080426
835511LV00016B/2556